Adding Depth To Your Destiny

**Deeper Insights Into
Life In Christ**

Volume 1

**By

Candi MacAlpine**

Adding Depth to Your Destiny
Copyright © 2014
Candi MacAlpine

All rights reserved. No part of this publication may be reproduced, stored in a retrieval system, or transmitted in any form or by any means—electronic, mechanical, photocopying, recording, or otherwise—without the prior written permission of the publisher and copyright owner. The only exception is brief quotations in printed reviews.

7710-T Cherry Park Drive, Suite 224
Houston, TX 77095
(281) 830-8724

Eddie@SpiriTruthPublishing.com
http://www.SpiriTruthPublishing.com

Printed in the United States of America

EBook: 978-1-304-98534-7

Softcover: 978-0692209691

Hardcover: 978-1-304-98532-3

Contents

Endorsement 7

Foreword 9

Introduction 11

Day 1 18

Day 2 19

Day 3 21

Day 4 23

Day 5 25

Day 6 26

Day 7 28

Day 8 30

Day 9 33

Day 10 34

Day 11 36

Day 12 38

Day 13 40

Day 14 42

Day 15 44

Day 16 47

Day 17 49

Day 18 51

Day 19 53

Day 20 55

Day 21 58

Day 22 60

Day 23 61

Day 24 63

Day 25 65

Day 26 69

Day 27 71

Day 28 73

Day 29 75

Day 30 77

Day 31 79

Day 32 80

Day 33 82

Day 34..84

Day 35..86

Day 36..88

Day 37..92

Day 38..96

Day 39..98

Day 40..101

Bibliography...104

About the Author...105

Other Books Written by the Author 106

Endorsement

"I highly recommend this book of 40 days of brief devotional contemplations based on solid prophetic words. As the title suggests, the reader will be moved deeper and closer to his or her personal destiny and the Lord's will and heart."

Doris Wagner, Minister
Global Spheres, Inc.

Foreword

Life is hard. Regardless of who you are, where you live, or your circumstances, life is a challenge. This is true even for those of us who've centered our lives on the Lord Jesus Christ and His Word.

When I was still a teenager I entered full-time evangelism and began traveling the U.S. conducting concerts, crusades and revival meetings. Some people may have thought mine was "a dream job." However, what they didn't know was that those days on the road were often lonely. What I longed for most was a mentor. Because I ministered from the platform night after night, many looked to me for wisdom and insight. Oh how I longed for a mentor from whom I could receive wisdom and insight.

My dear friend Candi MacAlpine is a godly, gifted, spiritually-mature woman of God. In a day when mentors are hard to find, I consider Candi "a treasure trove of spiritual wealth." Consider yourself fortunate for having found this wonderful book.

Frankly, I like 30-day and 40-day books like this one. Most of us are very busy people. Books like this offer us "bite-size," manageable, easy-to-read and to process gems. This book lives up to its title. As you read, it will help shape, and add depth to your destiny.

Interestingly, 100 or more years ago, what we speak of today as the "deeper life," was referred to and known as the "higher life." Whatever you prefer to call it, it's the victorious and abundant life in Christ we are called to live. Yet many in the church lack understanding of their spiritual gifts, their purpose, or their destiny.

Candi and I share similar passions. We have chosen to focus our lives on intimacy with the Son of God and we consider our calling to be that of discipling others.

I encourage you to allow Candi to speak into your life through the pages of this excellent book and in the next 40 days you will be transformed!

Dr. Alice Smith, Executive Director
U.S. Prayer Center
Houston, Texas

Introduction

What reverberates in our hearts with the desire to go deeper in our relationship and knowledge of the Father, Jesus the Son, and the Holy Spirit?

I believe it is resident in the deepest part of our being, even our DNA. On that finding I make this statement of our need, and desire to pursue personal growth to that fullness of our destiny.

Destiny is a very important word in my spiritual vocabulary, and I am passionate about seeing people fulfill their destiny in their generation. The Father has gifted me to see people's destiny, and speaking to that destiny as I encounter them. If I am not able to speak it, I will pray to the Father that it to come to pass. Nothing excites me more than to see an individual move step by step into the fullness of their destiny.

I have tried, but I cannot get away from this subject of *destiny*, so here we are again talking about destiny, but this time it is from the Father first. If you have read any of my other books, it is resident within the pages of those repeatedly.

Also found within the pages of this book are themes of *intimacy, faith,* and *revelation of the days to come*. Those seem to be the most prevalent.

This began about 2006 as a weekly prophetic word from the Father sent out by email every Monday. It was called *Monday Manna*. It was awesome to hear from the Father and then send it out to hundreds of people to start their week. It included direction, encouragement, and sometimes correction. Many forwarded each week's *Monday Manna* on to friends and family, and along the way I would find out or see them posted on a number of other websites, prophetic bulletin boards, and even on TV programs.

After about five years of releasing *Monday Manna* each week, the Lord revealed to me that the season had ended. Then several years later I began to hear "it is time to publish *Monday Manna* as a devotional for my body to use over and over and expand on each week's word by bringing understanding and expansion of its meaning." You can start anytime no matter the date on the calendar. It is intended to be used again and again.

I trust this will be a time of growth, destiny and purpose in your life. As always, I would love to hear the reports of its impact on you and others. I love hearing from my readers. It encourages me to keep to the path of impacting people that I would never meet. This is a 40 day journey you are about to embark on. It surely is unknown at this point for you, but I trust it will quickly unfold for you.

The number 40 is of great significance in Yahweh's Kingdom. In Kevin Conner's book *Interpreting the Symbols and Types* the number 40 is referenced in the following scriptures: Numbers 13:5; 14:33-34; Matthew 4:2; Acts 1:5; Exodus 34:27-28; Ezekiel 4:6; Acts 7:30; 1 Kings 10:4-8. Kevin states the number 40 represents "number of probation, testing, ending in victory or defeat."

In Paula Price's book *The Prophet's Dictionary* she writes regarding the number 40: "The number of spiritual preparation through trials and wilderness bouts. When applied to time it refers to a season predisposed to natural disaster and calamities.' Also, forty years is the length of time it takes Pleiades – the star cluster of the seven stars—to appear. Forty is an ancient number linked to purification and used in the Bible to commemorate significant events in the calendar of God. Whenever the number is employed prophetically, it is indicative of a dramatic, elongated act of the Almighty. Biblical events associated with the number forty are:

- The flood
- The Israelites wandering in the wilderness

- Moses and God's Sinai summit
- David and Solomon's rule
- Christ's wilderness temptation
- Christ's three and a half-year ministry
- Christ's forty-day post-resurrection ministry"

The importance of understanding the spiritual significance of numbers is valuable in seeing the fulfillment of destiny in your life.

Almost every day has a prophecy as the foundation for that day. It is italicized to stand out to the audience as to its importance.

I have referred to God in several of His names in this devotional. I want you to understand that God is not a name but a function. Yahweh and Jehovah are some of the names of the creator of the universe. We want to call him by his name and not his function.

He is a personal God who desires personal relationship with his creation and desires to be called by His name, of which there are hundreds.

I did not want you to be confused by this so I wanted to communicate it to you from the beginning. If you want to understand more about the names of our God then I would highly suggest the book *His Glorious Names* by Rev. Quamaniq and Dr. Suuqiina. They write of 365 names of YHWH and all the significance of each name. You can order it from their website *Indigenous Messengers International*. It is a necessity for every Christian's bookshelf in my opinion. It will change your understanding of the God we serve. It covers the Hebrew letters and their meanings, the musical notes, because every Hebrew letter is also a note and the biblical passages.

In my first book *Take Back the Night* as an Appendix I listed the more than 200 names of our God compiled by Dr. Sam Sasser, a wonderful man of Jehovah and missionary to the Micronesian Islands for many years. He is now in glory with the One who created and loves him. He compiled that list over 20 years of experience and research.

Day 1

See the new day and new year that is dawning before you, the day I have made, and it is good and you can rejoice that I have great things planned for you this day and the days to come, days of joy, days of destiny, days to remember all that I have done for and in you, days to see the Kingdom advanced and many coming into the Kingdom. Be not afraid of those past things that have hung you up before, because it is a new day and my mercies are new each morning. I have reserved for you this day my peace and my presence as you step into that place of secrecy to meet with me each day. I love and desire to spend time with you, come be with me today my child.

These 40 days will represent a significant change in your life, start it off right, with faith, and with excitement that the one who loves you best is taking your hand and will lead you down this path of great growth, great new experiences, great new levels of intimate relationship with your Bridegroom.

Day 2

Destiny—what is it? The New Living translation has several passages that will help us.

Dan 5:23 *"But you have not honored the God who gives you the breath of life and controls your destiny!"*

Job 23:14 *"So he will do to me whatever he has planned. He controls my destiny."*

Ps 73:24 *"You guide me with your counsel, leading me to a glorious destiny."*

Eccl 6:10b *"So there's no use arguing with God about your destiny."*

Webster's 1828 Dictionary of the English Language describes destiny as: "the state or condition appointed or predetermined; ultimate fate; as men are solicitous to know their future destiny, which is however happily concealed from them".

Back in 1828 Noah Webster was letting us know that destiny was a word that needed to be defined so that people would pursue that which was concealed and that which had been revealed.

Write 3 things that have been revealed to you regarding your destiny then declare them out loud over yourself.

1.

2.

3.

Day 3

Jer. 29:11-13

"For I know the plans I have for you," says the Lord. "They are plans for good and not for disaster, to give you a future and a hope," says the Lord. "They are plans for good and not for disaster, to give you a future and a hope. 12 In those days when you pray, I will listen. 13 you look for me wholeheartedly, you will find me.

In this passage Yahweh is declaring His truth over you and telling you His plan and it is all good and he promises hope and a future (or destiny). It is a promise, not words in the wind by someone who cannot keep their promises. Israel had spent 60 years in captivity before this, due to their rebellion and disobedience to the word of Jehovah. In spite of their rebellion He promises to restore them as they cry out to him in humility and repentance for their rebellion. It is no different for us, we have all rebelled, and we have all disobeyed. Scripture is very clear that all of us have sinned and fallen way short of His glorious purpose. But over and over again Yahweh promises to restore us to him, so let this be that day when you humble yourself under His mighty hand

and say "here I am, transform me into my destiny and purpose, I am yours."

Declare this passage today, in fact write it or print it out and put it on your refrigerator or wherever you will see it most and leave it there for *the 40 days of destiny* and see where you are at the end of the 40 days.

Day 4

One of the biggest hindrances or obstructions to destiny is fear, and the Lord makes it very clear in this prophecy to not be afraid.

2 Tim. 1:7 "For God has not given us a spirit of fear and timidity, but of power, love, and self-discipline."

Yahweh is clear in this passage that fear is a demonic spirit and it has not been given to us by God, but what has been given to us is power, love and self-discipline to pursue and succeed in fulfilling our destiny in our generation.

If there is fear lurking at your door, or even overtaking you, write down each fear and then begin to declare the word of Yahweh over yourself breaking that stronghold of fear and sending it back to the pit of hell. And after you have done that take a big black marker and obliterate each one as an act of FAITH. If it takes you a while to do this, no problem, just be sure to do it and eradicate every fear.

You may have overlooked another spirit and that is timidity and it is not part of the Christian's life and destiny, so repent and cast them out. Tell them not to darken your doors ever again, and move forward into the next day of your destiny.

Day 5

Mercy, mercy, mercy! We could not live on this planet without the mercy of our God each day.

Lam. 3:23-24

"Great is his faithfulness; his mercies begin afresh each morning. 24 I say to myself, "The Lord is my inheritance; therefore, I will hope in him!"

The word inheritance here is big. There is not enough space here to discuss it fully, but it would be a great word study. Each one of us has been promised an inheritance as a child of Yahweh and mercy for every day. That tells me that we must need mercy every day, so let's appropriate it in our pursuit of our destiny, and cry out for it, thank Him for it, and declare it to the heavens that "I have mercy fresh and new today for whatever I encounter."

Day 6

Would you believe I am a God that does not speak? I guarantee that the false gods and idols do not speak nor can they for they are not gods at all. I am that I am and I speak and have always spoken to that which I have created for my glory. I desire to speak intimately with you every day. I await the time for you to come be by my side and listen so that I may declare to you that which is true and that which is of your destiny. Look to my word and see again and again that I have spoken to my children and even those who have turned their back on me. I am a communicator at all times and desire that you would be a listener of my words as we sit in the secret place and even in that place where there is a whirlwind surrounding you. Be not afraid for I am one who will show you the path and direction and give you guidance and yes as a loving father I will correct and discipline you but it will always be to see you move to a new place in me and your destiny.

The key to every relationship we have is *communication*. Without *communication* there is no relationship. You cannot become intimate at any level unless you communicate. It may be words, it may be sign language or even brail, but without it there will be no moving forward to a higher or deeper level of communication let alone a deeper level of intimacy and relationship. We must first and foremost believe that Yahweh does speak. Well you might say of course He speaks, look at the Bible, and I would respond of course He has spoken through His word, but He also speaks to what He has created, in nature, in weather, in art, in our hearts and through His prophets as well as prophetic people. We must begin here to move deeper into this intimate relationship and our destiny and to simply listen. I promise you He will speak.

Sometimes it is that we are too busy doing, and we need to stop, sit down, and listen. Listen as Elijah did for the still small voice.

1 Kings 19:11-13 *"Go out and stand before me on the mountain," the Lord told him. And as Elijah stood there the Lord passed by, and a mighty windstorm hit the mountain; it was such a terrible blast that the rocks were torn loose, but the Lord was not in the wind. After the wind, there was an earthquake, but the Lord was not in the earthquake. 12 And after the earthquake, there was a fire, but the Lord was not in the fire. And after the fire, there was the sound of a gentle whisper. 13 When Elijah heard it, he wrapped his face in his scarf and went out and stood at the entrance of the cave.*

Day 7

The fire is heating up can you feel it. Do not be afraid of it but embrace it. What it contains for you first and foremost is Me, for I AM A CONSUMING FIRE, and I cannot be quenched. This fire is to burn away everything that is standing in my way either hiding or concealing my glory in you. I want to see you fired up, I want to see this generation all as firebrands marking territories and marking nations and marking my Kingdom. This is an hour for all of every generation to look to my word on their own to press forward to that place of significance in time and in their generation no matter their age. My fire shall reveal the gold, my fire shall stir the whirlwind to dispose of every bit of debris cluttering my Kingdom, for my kingdom is holy. Do not be discouraged even though you struggle with your own inward thoughts and feelings, for the blood of my Son has washed away into the ocean of forgiveness and forgetting all things. I will use each vessel that will be willing and say yes to my calling. I will supply everything that is needed along the way and at the exact time. Remember, do not box me in time, for I do not function in time for eternity has no time.

Usually we do not like fire, unless it is warming our cold bodies. But in this instance, Jehovah has a fire that we have not seen, only Moses saw it burning but not burning up anything, a holy fire, on holy ground. Today is the day to let the holy fire of heaven rain down and consume all that would be burned to cinder and see only the gold that remains. Your destiny is wrought with fire and cleansing and restoring all things, because He is a God of restoration. Embrace the fire today and let it burn, remembering it will not harm you but only inspire you toward your destiny.

Day 8

There are some who are living in dread and fear and there are others who are living in prosperity and tranquility. There will always be those but I say that my kingdom is of love, grace, peace, mercy, forgiveness, hope, destiny, purpose, abiding, authority, giving, receiving, vision, living, multiplying, seeing and many other attributes that bring my creation to new heights in relationship to me. Would you look at creation all around you and see the order and submission it has to my purposes? Look at the animals that are in complete order in their existence. I have created all of this for you to rule and reign over, here and now, and also in eternity in the new world yet to come. This is your training ground; this is your preparation of training for reigning and for getting all the kinks out before the great and terrible day of the Lord yet to come. I am speaking strongly again of things yet to come, but I must first have the body of Christ in order to co labor more fully in the purposes of my Kingdom says your God. My kingdom is not of one nation or another or one people group or another or one social economic group or another, my kingdom is unfathomable, it is not just this earth but all of the universe and solar systems and even beyond that and it is also a spiritual realm that your parents Adam and Eve gave up when their eyes were opened and they ate of the tree of the knowledge of good and evil. You must be people of the spirit walking in the kingdom, one easily seen and the other not so easily seen or understood, but my Spirit will teach and train and open your eyes to this realm so that you will have the fullness of understanding of both these realms to establish the Kingdom of God throughout your known world and bring transformation to all peoples and all places.

Yahweh's kingdom is real, we carry it within us, and we are to establish it daily, knowing it is with His authority that we do. It is part of our destiny to do this. It is part of our purpose here on this earth. My faith is always encouraged when I look at creation around me. I live in the High Sierras of California, outside the southern gate to Yosemite National Park. We love living here, and it is a constant reminder to me of the creator and how creation is in perfect obedience to the order and plan of Jehovah. I personally need that, and it also builds me up knowing my destiny is like unto nature except on a much higher level and a level of personal relationship with that creator.

I want to complete my training here on earth so that I can fully reign with Jesus in eternity. We must look at each intersection of life as part of that training, and make the correct choice at that intersection to go forward in our destiny quest.

Might I suggest to you a very simple, exercise? Find somewhere you can go and take a road trip to where creation surrounds you, take a chair, and find a quiet place and sit quietly for an extended period of time, and watch and listen. I promise you will be overwhelmed as you purpose to look with your own eyesight at the beauty of what Yahweh has created for us to remind us of His plan and purpose and write down what you hear him saying, write down some desires you have in regard to your destiny. You might even take a picnic and spend the day.

Day 9

According to my word, and my plan, I have desired for every generation to take their rightful place in my eternal purpose on this earth and ultimately eternity. Every time discouragement comes knocking on your door, do not answer the door and put up the closed sign. Turn and walk into my presence and my word and you will find solace for your soul and your day.

We have tried so hard to put Yahweh in a box and He will not stay there, which is very frustrating for us when we function in religion and not in relationship. He created the universe beyond anything we could ever imagine, why would we think we could pin him within a box of our making and design? He will not do it, so we might as well, throw that box in the fire and let it burn and look up, as He told Abraham to see what lies ahead, a generation of world changers shining brightly across the beautiful expanse of our world. You are one of them!

Day 10

Do you know how well I know you? Before you were even conceived I already had you in my heart and plan. A plan for a people one by one who would love me, walk with me in the cool of the evening, and be my glory in the earth. I have not changed my plan or purpose for you, so why are you questioning who you are and what you are here on this earth for? Is it because of the circumstances in your life? I will use all things to bring you up higher into the realms of the spirit so that I can reveal to you more and more about myself and the Kingdom I have created. You will see it completed. I have an exact fit for you in my body and everyone has a perfect place and each of you is most important. I cannot do without any one of you. You are needed in order to see the Kingdom of God come into the earth realm and be established. Be assured I am working in every area of your life. Do not look downward but look upward into my face and you will then be able to press forward.

How will He do this? Well since it is His plan we might as well submit to the plan, and watch it unfold, one day at a time. Place your hand in His hand and walk. Walking is forward movement. It is not stagnant, it is not stationery, it is life going from what has already taken place to a place that has not been before. We all do it, but we don't think much about it as we are doing it. Take a walk today, and this time think about your forward movement. In its simplest form you are moving forward into your destiny by the simple act of walking. Now apply it spiritually and talk with someone; write about it. I believe you will smile.

Day 11

My child, I want you to take a moment and pause and look at your hands. I created them as a tool of the gospel, a tool that you may or may not have understood their spiritual significance. They were created to reach out, to touch and caress giving my love and acceptance; they were created as tools of praise and worship and to be tools of warfare to defeat the enemy. They were also created to open doors in the natural that would take you to places and people you would not have expected. Be sure these tools are kept clean and not used for destruction, and hurting people, and rejecting that which I have said is good. If these hands become less than holy, use them to turn the pages of my word taking the water of my word and wash them, cleansing them and restoring them to their rightful place. Use these hands to proclaim and declare the glory of my kingdom and my son. Use them lifted to worship and praise me. Use them to wrap around the one who is hurting and in despair. Use them to reach out and feed the poor and care for the orphans of so many circumstances. They are one of the most used parts of your body, my temple, the residence of the Holy Spirit. Make a vow to me today to use them for nothing but my Kingdom and my purposes.

I believe this is self-explanatory. Might I suggest a word study on the topic of "hands," especially in scripture? I promise you that it will amaze you.

Day 12

Beloved, do your tears keep you from moving onward and upward? Remember that I am sensitive to the tears you shed and I keep them within the realms of heaven in bottles created to hold them for all eternity. It is not only a poetic portion of my word, but is significant to your knowledge of not only my love but of knowing the deepest and most difficult times of your life. I also am aware of those times of great joy. I created your body and its tears so be not afraid as the fall for they fall right into my hands.

Take some time to *really* think about your tears. The Scripture that tells us our heavenly Father saves our tears in a bottle is not simply poetic writing. It was written by the Holy Spirit and directed from the Father through human hands on earth. Can you imagine what they thought when they received that revelation. Meditate on this a while and I believe you, like they, will be speechless.

What power do they hold on you and your destiny? In reality they do not, but if you have allowed them to hinder your destiny journey, then it's time to repent and then move onward, letting those tears fall right into His hands.

Day 13

Sing unto the Lord a new song, I say sing unto me, do not look around you at your circumstances, or the condition of the earth, but sing unto me and watch the heavens part and the rain of my Spirit begin to descend over you and over regions and over cities and over nations. Yes, I say you can see people, places, and things change as you sing unto me. Let the praises of your mouth lift high the banner of my love and the banner of my power to see significant changes even in the atmosphere of the weather patterns that are arising and being distributed across the earth. I am that I am and I will not be thwarted from my sovereignty upon the earth or even the universe. Man says we have found this and we have found that and now this and such is true, but I say nothing has changed, what was and is still are and my truth never changes and my truth will be confirmed as man comes across those things I decide will be confirmed. I speak to the world and say look to my word for in it are the issues of life and death and eternity and every word is true and there is no lie and there is no confusion and there is no compromise and there is no conflict. Line upon line and precept upon precept, all is penned by my hand across the universe and my word will prevail against anything man or devil would try and purport to be truth when it is not. Remember he that comes in the night comes but to steal, kill and destroy and he is a liar and the father of lies. Do not be deceived by his crafty ways and lust of the eyes and lust of the flesh and lust for power and the things of this world. For I say soon it will all end and I will begin a new age, a new world and eternity like has not been seen by the eyes of man, only those who have come before me down through the ages and now know. Remember the man who chose hell and went and saw his brothers and wanted to go tell them and my word declares they have all seen and been told the truth and they have not embraced it. For I tell you this day that TRUTH is and was and always will be and it will prevail in this hour even at the high courts of this land and even in the government offices and even at the Pentagon my truth will be introduced and man will see and be amazed.

Wow, the magnitude of the power of God's voice across the waters shifts creation to stand at attention, and so should we. His Kingdom will stand forever. All other things will burn into wood, hay and stubble. We have a life and an eternity like none other and one day we will be amazed at what we did not know. Please don't be a hearer of the word only. Be a doer of the word. Be a student of that word, be a lover of that word, be a disciple of that word, be the Christ follower He has called you to be, receiving and believing the truth He has brought forth to you.

Day 14

My child, how many times do you feel that I am not listening or that I am not there or that I am not speaking to you? You must know that I am never away from you and I would never leave or forsake you. There are times in me when what seems real to you is really not, it can be an assignment from the enemy or it can be my pressing you to walk in a higher level of faith. If the enemy has thwarted your sense of my presence, begin to worship me and He will flee immediately. You are as close to me as your next breath and I know everything about you and I also listen to you and I am always speaking to you, through my word, through the still small voice and through the prophetic and through walking in the spirit. Become so accustomed to hearing my voice that you never doubt its existence and its constant presence in and around you.

I AM says I am always listening. He knows the smallest thing about us and every little desire and plan we have. He also is that great Dad who smiles when he sees how little things can so create havoc in our day. He knows tomorrow will be better and you will grow and mature and one day he will see you in all your maturity being all he knew you would be.

Take some time today to sit and listen. Psa. 46:10 be still and know I am God.

Day 15

Some days it feels as if you have an open window to heaven and to my throne. And some days it feels as if the heavens are as brass. But why would you ever think I am not right here with you on the good days and the bad days. It is not by emotion that you know I am close at hand; it is by faith, the faith that passes all understanding. It is the faith that really does move mountains, the faith that is only the size of a mustard seed, but when it is fully complete is a huge tree. Do you not realize that I am with you all the time, and yes I do hear your cry and I do hear every prayer you pray, even though at times it is in desperation, as if I really do not exist. Know that the world is coming to its finish and things are accelerating in all arenas and the enemy is trying a last ditch affect on the kingdom, but he will fail miserably and will not fulfill his desire upon my church and my purposes for those who have yet to come into the kingdom. Let your faith be increased this day, for it is a gift and a fruit, double time, allow it to invade your mind, your will, your emotions, your spirit and watch its manifestation take place where you least expect it.

Why is it we , like the dog that returns to its vomit, as Proverbs says, fall back into that "stinkin' thinkin'" that our heavenly Father would ever not be there, would not hear our hearts cry? His word is clear on this. How many times does He tell us in His word that He is always there? If he saves every tear we cry in bottles then certainly He is intimately acquainted with everything about us. Remember He created us and according to Psa. 139 he knew every day of our life before there was even one day. He has the ability to bring us closer and closer to our destiny in the most unusual ways, ways in which we are about to give up, and our faith is at the bottom of the barrel and the glass is not just half-empty, it is down to its last drop. I have lived long enough on this planet to see that He has NEVER failed me, always showed up, and always brought me through to the other side.

Something I have learned in my process is that the enemy will try to convince you that this will never change and it will never end. Well that is not the truth, everything ends and things have to change because that is the way it works. There is a season for everything, in the natural and in the spirit.

Take some time to look at the seasons of your life. They are very prophetic in the naturalness of the creation, each season speaks for itself, be it fall when things are beginning to drop off and things are beginning to look bare, and all the green and flowers have died, followed by winter where it seems everything is dead, but in the secret place sap is flowing, and growth is being prepared, and new blossoms and fruit are being formed in the DNA of the plant to bring forth in the time of harvest food to fill the body. The spring brings joy as everything bursts forth out of what looks like death and everywhere creation sings of a new season of life, followed by summer where the warmth of the sun brings peace and hope for the next cycle of seasons in creation and in our lives and destiny.

Journal here what you are realizing…..

Day 16

Stand and be amazed at what I am about to do in your life. It is around the corner. The problem with corners is that you are walking one way and cannot see around it. You will be amazed, surprised, and full of faith as you choose to walk to the corner and make the turn. Life has been filled with intersections and corners for which you may choose to cross, change, or even make the turn. I have set myself as one who wants to release greater and greater levels of faith so you can walk in more confidence and take the turns that I avail to you. My walk is not a difficult walk in the sense of trusting me. It is a walk that requires you to count the cost before beginning the journey, but it is a walk that requires absolute obedience, trust, and faith. But I have given to you the gift of faith and the fruit of faith and I have given you my word again and again from beginning to end that speaks specifically of obedience and faith. The life of my son on earth was the fullness of obedience, trust and faith and it proved to all who would see and believe that all things are possible with me.

We need to be reminded that goodness and mercy follow us and that Yahweh's plans for us are for success and a future that is good, no matter what we see with our natural eye. No matter what emotion I feel, it is not the true test of what is planned by the mighty God of the universe when I chose to follow hard after him no matter what the surrounding circumstances look like. Each opportunity the Father places in our hands is a place for our faith to increase. He loves increasing our faith because it makes us more like Jesus and gives us greater and greater opportunity to exercise the authority of the Kingdom on earth, defeating our enemy's plans to steal, kill and destroy us. Allow Him to remind you today and watch it unfold.

Day 17

Are their days my child when you feel on top of the world and know where you're going and what you are going to do, and at peace with my will and plan for your life? Then are their days when you feel the world is on top of you, crushing you and your spirit, and you have no peace and have no idea what you are to do and what my plan is for your life? My child know without any doubt that I never change and I never have struggles and I never wonder what my plan is, for I am the beginning and the end, I know the first from the last. I created everything, I say everything that exists on this earth I created, and I called it good and I have a perfect plan and it will not fail. Be assured it will not fail, and everything I have written in my word will come to pass, and every plan and purpose I have for you is waiting for you to say yes, for you to rise up in the faith I have given you and even more faith, if you ask for it, and you will see the Son, moon, and stars rejoice along with the angelic hosts in heaven for when one man or woman or child says yes to me it can change history. It can change a people; it can change a nation, even in one day if I deem it so. So what are you waiting for? I have heroes of the Kingdom waiting to take hold of the prophecies of the ages and say yes to the Kingdom and yes to my plan that will succeed and will not fail and yes no matter the stumbling blocks and no matter the opposition; I will not fail in you.

Sometimes our Father has to speak strongly like an earthly father wanting to communicate something very important, something the child needs to hear in order for them to mature in some level. I did not have a father growing up so I have clung to my heavenly father and He has become everything to me as that father and I know all things will work together for my good because He loves me and He has chosen the best for me. I must listen, and take action and realize not by my understanding but by what Father says to be true and will be accomplished by His hand.

Take some time today to mediate on these words and let them go deep into your heart and Spirit, let them wash away any mindsets that are in opposition to His desire and will for you in this season.

Day 18

I will no longer tolerate idols in hearts, minds or buildings that claim to be God. I alone am God and I will have no other gods before me says the Lord and I will bring a sword and a flood against them in days to come for I am that I am and I am the alpha and the omega, the beginning and the end of all things. And in this hour I will show myself in ways not seen for many a century, for child know that the time is short, really short, and I am raising up an army like never before and I have positioned angels throughout the earth who are eager to be released by my hand to come battle and do the work of the Kingdom that will be released from the throne and the council of heaven in this hour.

We are his workmanship created for His glory on this earth and for all eternity. I always say you must have an eternal perspective to make it through this time on earth. It is a time in the earth where Jehovah is moving like no other time and we are His instruments on this earth to bring vengeance against anything that tries to hinder or stop the works of Jehovah on this earth. We are an army as His church and Jesus' bride and all that entails.

Today journal what this means to you and also look to see if there are any hidden 'idols' lurking around that need to be told to take a hike. This temple is for Yahweh and Yahweh alone.

Day 19

You are my threshing instruments, sharp and clean, ready to take off the heads of any who try and rise up any other standard than my standard says the Lord. Be wise as serpents but gentle like a dove in your warfare, for it will take much wisdom and council and even love to walk like the mighty warriors I have raised up throughout history. When it comes to the enemy take no captives, but you must be very discerning as to what the enemy is and what he is not. For your battle is not against flesh and blood, but against the powers and principalities and hosts of wickedness in high places. For too long many have battled against their brothers and sisters and I say stop, and again I say it must stop and you must put on the armor of God, with the helmet of salvation, girding your loins with truth, placing the breastplate of righteousness on your chest, shod your feet with the gospel of peace, and taking up the shield of faith and the sword of the spirit which is my word, ready to be like Joshua and take no captives, but at times I will allow you the spoils of the battle for the expansion of my kingdom purposes.

You must realize we are in a war and it will not end until King Jesus returns on that great white Steed with the sword in His hand and written on His thigh *King of*

Kings, and Lord of Lords. He will take no prisoners and He will win. In reality He has won, He did it on the cross, and nothing can reverse or limit or diminish it. He has provided for us the armor of God and it is Himself and we are able because He says so. So take a look at your armor and check it out and remind yourself who He is and who He says you are and rise up and take the land in your homes, your families, your cities, your nations.

Day 20

TODAY marks the half-way point of these 40 days of *Adding Depth to Your Destiny*. I pray you have come a long way since day 1 and you are ready to move past the half-way point to see what the next 20 days holds for you. I am excited for you and I am praying for you to see with new eyes, experience Him and His Kingdom in new ways and realize you are a force to be reckoned with on this earth and that the hordes of hell are becoming terrified of you and your authority and your place in God's Kingdom.

I have told you in long times past and again today that you are to know the times and the seasons and know by the spirit what is taking place in the kingdom. I tell you today that there is much ready to tumble out of the spirit realm into reality seen by the eyes of man. I have for centuries revealed myself to the prophets and many have risen up in these past days and you have even grown weary of their musings, but I tell you that each one knows in part and prophesies in part and together is a bigger picture. Stand back in the place where you are and look at a bigger picture, seek my face as to the bigger picture. Do not be dismayed by what some would say for I say that my ways are not your ways and my thoughts are not your thoughts and I am working in greater ways than you realize and I am beginning to prepare the way for a new year is arising and in that place will come many a thing of Kingdom power, authority, and presence. Find that new or deeper place in me before this year ends for the new year, a year of great revelation is upon you and upon my church and I am about to speak forth through many a voice, even voices you would not expect to hear from me, be sensitive to my spirit and discern that which is of me and that which is not says your God. I am on the scene, hear me, I am on the scene in places you would not expect me to be and I am working a greater miracle than you would expect and in places you would not expect to see my miracles break forth into the midst of what seems like great evil has taken over, for I say I am God and there is no other, and I will be exalted in ALL the earth and I will turn the hearts of many whose hearts have grown cold and have hardened by the world and its system that says there is no God and He does not intervene in the lives of mankind, for I say I created all and everything and I will see my glory manifested in this earth and in the earth to come. Be knowing that evil is seemingly getting stronger because I am about to overtake evil and bring light where great darkness has prevailed for many a season. It is the day of my arrival on the scene and the scene will now change and you will be amazed, says your God.

This half-way mark is a defining point for you to evaluate how far you have come and how much you really have accomplished. I am convinced that you have come further than you realize and that you can now see that you have come to the top of the mountain and the remaining days of adding depth to your destiny is a reality and it is bearing fruit you have not seen yet, but it has produced more than you realize, so rise up in new energy of faith and purpose for your greatest days are before you.

Day 21

There are days my child when it seems like there is a whirlwind moving around you and confusion comes knocking at the door and you struggle with even everyday things of life. I tell you and promised you and continue to promise you that there will always be times when things around you will vie for your attention and want to overwhelm you and take control of you, but I say that I am there to put things in perspective and as you walk by my spirit you will get the proper perspective of any and all things that vie for my place of attention and the attention of my Kingdom followers. Even now during this season keep your eyes on Jesus and know that it is not only a season to focus on Him, but you are to put all things into His care for He cares for you. You will see those things just not have any affect. They may not stop and they may not change but you can see with different eyes and respond with different responses so that as a kingdom dweller you are the one in charge with my Spirit guiding you each day and in every circumstance.

The key word here is perspective. You must have His perspective. You have tried too long with your own perspective, and as Dr. Phil says, "How's that workin' for you?"

Jehovah's perspective is permanent and will go on throughout all eternity, and you have the awesome privilege and opportunity to tune into His perspective. I promise it will change your life up in ways so incredible you will have a hard time believing it. Remember Prov. 3:5-6, *"Trust in the Lord with all your might, and do not lean on your own understanding. In all your ways acknowledge Him and He will make your path straight."* It behooves us to take His word at face value and to believe it and act upon it each time we come across specific *rhemas* that explode in our hearts and minds (really our spirits). The reason they impact us so strongly is for that very reason of us realizing we need to take action on that word.

Let this be a new day for you to take stock of perspective, Yahweh's perspective, and take action on it.

Day 22

See this day that you heed and hear and take action on your knees to my command. My generals are waiting for you to come up next to them and heed their instructions that have come from me and are from the council of heaven. They have been waiting and pressing in for some time now and they like I have need of you in this hour, no longer are you to be complacent and apathetic, it is a time of war and a time of victory and a time for prophetic utterances to be manifested and completed in the earth says your God.

There is a really good reason Jehovah gave us two ears. It was so we could have two orifices to hear what was being said either by others or by him. It's a simple principle; hear and obey. Keep track of what you hear and your responses and the results of those responses.

Take some time today to sit again and listen. Something jaw dropping may make an impact on your life, or it might just be the realization of His great love and passion for you. Remember you are his favorite!

Day 23

My child, if you will confess your sins I am faithful and will forgive your sins and cleanse you from all unrighteousness. I am a father who loves to see the very best in my children, and I also know that sin is always lurking at your feet to ensnare you and pull you down, but I have provided a way, I have provided an escape, I have provided the answer for all sins; none is without the power of my love to forgive. Know that you and those you come in contact with are all as my word says not without sin but I have provided the very best redemption through the blood of my son Jesus, so begin today to tell those I bring to you that I love them and I do all things well and will for them also.

Today is a day to remember that the blood of Jesus has washed away your sin for all eternity. But also we want to please him and not disappoint him and sin, but when we do we can say thank you for the forgiveness that came through the blood of his son Jesus Christ, and thank you there is no condemnation toward me because I am hidden in Christ, the one who paid for all my sin when he went to the cross.

Take some time today to thank him for your forgiveness and that you are no longer under the law, but under grace, and that you have a great high priest who is interceding for you this very moment. Worship him for an extended period of time and receive that beautiful spirit of adoption afresh into His Kingdom.

Day 24

See the wonders of my universe. They were created to speak to you of the wonders of My Kingdom. They fly in the face of man who does not know me as they try and explain away My creation. But I tell you the wonders explain creation and what I have done in ages past. When everything around you is coming apart look to the universe and it speaks of things to come. Has not my word spoken of these things, has it not given you great wisdom to look to? I have many things in store for you in the seasons to come and they include all that is around you that can be seen with the naked eye and with the eye that has been created to look further. Look ahead in the days to come for astounding revelations from the universe that I have reserved for this time in the universe. They will speak of things I have already said and they will reveal that which has been in my word for ages. Simply look up and see the skies and be encouraged.

Sometimes we do not see what is right in front of our face. The world around us shouts revelation. It is so familiar to us that we forget to realize it was created with 1 word by the creator. Look at the majesty of it all, the hues of colors, the perfectness, the order of each leaf on a tree, the massive variety of flowers and the color range of those individual flowers. Take today and go someplace and see what is around you. Also wait till the nighttime and then go outside and look up at the majesty of the night sky, the stars, the galaxies; it takes your breath away and reminds us of the hugeness and the magnificence of our heavenly Father. Realize who you are as a child of the King of the universe.

Day 25

Can you feel the rain, can you see the rain, can you hear the rain, and can you smell the rain? I have created your senses to be sensitive to natural things and to spiritual things. You must train them so that you sense and respond to what I am speaking in this hour upon the earth and this time in the history of my Kingdom says your God. I created the rain; it first came to bring an end to the sin of man that was upon the earth. It is a powerful force that transcends man's ability to foresee. It then came to water the earth and cause things to grow and produce a harvest to feed man and beast alike. It has brought life to many and is a necessity to the life of man; without it you will die. I now say take this into the Spirit and see that it is no different there. I have and am sending the rain of my spirit upon the earth as my Prophet Joel prophesied, and at times it is and will be a gentle mist, and at times it will be a gentle rain where you can dance and rejoice and then there will be and are times of torrential rain that washes away all dirt and filth and even uproots things that have shallow roots and are not established deep into the soil of the Kingdom. It is a time for the rains of God to begin to manifest in cities and regions and yes even nations for the transformation that needs to come. It shall even wash away the camp of the enemy and leave it cleansed and pure. Think my child of how it smells after the rain has ended, see with spiritual eyes this manifestation upon the earth that is ever before you and realize this is a great spiritual principle, study it, pray about it, look to my word for the times there and the prophecies speaking forth for Israel as well as the Gentiles. Begin to see, hear, and smell with new understanding what I am speaking today, because the rain is beginning to fall in a new way; watch for its manifestations and walk in its fullness. Yes the rain of heaven is falling over your circumstances and it is a season to preserve the rain of my spirit in a spiritual barrel to drink from in the days of drought that certainly will follow for the time of man is coming to an end and the time of Jesus' return is upon you. Drink deeply of my rain my child, drink deeply, and be satisfied.

Equipping and training are very important for the children of Jehovah's kingdom. Ephesians makes it quite clear.

Eph. 4:11-16

"Now these are the gifts Christ gave to the church: the apostles, the prophets, the evangelists, and the pastors and teachers. 12 Their responsibility is to equip God's people to do his work and build up the church, the body of Christ. 13 This will continue until we all come to such unity in our faith and knowledge of God's Son that we will be mature in the Lord, measuring up to

the full and complete standard of Christ.14 Then we will no longer be immature like children. We won't be tossed and blown about by every wind of new teaching. We will not be influenced when people try to trick us with lies so clever they sound like the truth. 15 Instead, we will speak the truth in love, growing in every way more and more like Christ, who is the head of his body, the church. 16 He makes the whole body fit together perfectly. As each part does its own special work, it helps the other parts grow, so that the whole body is healthy and growing and full of love."

The truth herein is clear, Jehovah has provided the five-fold ministry of *apostles, prophets, evangelists, pastors* and *teachers*, to train and equip *us* for the work of the ministry, for the work of our destiny.

Our destiny is not some flighty childish playtime, but key for the kingdom of God to advance and for us to fulfill our destiny in our generation, as the word also speaks. Each generation is responsible to get trained and prepared to do the work of the ministry and to measure up to the standard Jesus Christ has given us. We each are an integral part of the body of Christ, and we cannot be replaced by another. It is a perfectly matched puzzle piece for us, so we have no excuses. It is right here in black and white, even red in places.

I challenge you to evaluate where you are at this juncture in being equipped and trained. We are so blessed by the apostolic and prophetic movements that are doing this very thing, preparing the saints in every arena of ministry and then sending each one out to do their ministry inside and outside of the corporate body of Christ. We are his handiwork, his workmanship and he has made us well and he clearly says so. I repeat we have no excuses for not pursuing our destiny.

If you need training and equipping, get on a computer and Google "Christian training." Many will arise including: *Christian International Apostolic Network, Wagner Leadership Institute, Encounters Network,* and so many others, large and small, and there are so many online capabilities.

We have a smorgasbord of training at our fingertips. So put your fingers to walking, not through *The Yellow Pages,* as in days of old, but on your computer keyboard and see what unfolds for you, always praying before to be directed by the Holy Spirit to what fits for you.

Day 26

Do you not know that my heart is always, always, always turned toward you and every need and every concern that is uppermost in your heart and mind? You are never out of my thoughts and my desire is to see you succeed in all you endeavor to do, for I am the God of success, but remember I have an understanding of success that is not like the world's and is only of the Kingdom so do not despair in all you have put your hands and heart toward for I am in the midst of it, and I am watching and working with you and the Holy Spirit is right by your side guiding you in each decision and turn. You are a delight to me and as you press forward into life I will always be there and will never forsake you my child.

I have to smile because we are so predictable in so many ways. We need reminding again and again how much Yahweh loves and cares for us, and our every thought. We are not ones who must take a number and wait our turn. It is always our turn, we are always number 1, and He is always waiting for us to turn to him for reassurance and his promises and his mercies that are new every morning.

So take some time today and sit in his presence and enjoy his predictable love and care and desire to see you fulfill his purpose and destiny for your life. I am sure you have noticed by now I use the word destiny a lot. It is an important word, and I have already shared its meanings and significance in each of our lives, so here is another opportunity to draw closer to our Lord and King and to be lifted up to see our significance to him and to the kingdom.

Day 27

It may seem to some to be the dark night of the soul, and your feelings, emotions and circumstances seem to cause your mind to feel that I am not on the scene, but I promise you my promises are true, such as I will never leave you or forsake you. Know that even when it feels like I am a long way off, I am really as close as your next breath and I know your heart and the things that you are struggling with and know that I will bring you out, and you will leave the desert for another time. I am that I am and all things work together for good for those called according to my purposes.

Take a deep breath, and I do not mean any kind of Yoga, and breathe in a fresh infilling of Jehovah's Spirit into your day and your circumstances. I am sure by this point the enemy of your soul has tried more than once to distract you from these 40 days of digging deep into your destiny. I do not doubt he has been trying to defeat you and told you more than one lie, but be strong in the power of Yahweh's might and walk in faith toward fulfilling what you began 27 days ago and see what unfolds and write them down.

The strategies the enemy tried on you during this time you will remember the next time he comes knocking on your door. We are clearly told by the apostle Paul to know the wiles of the enemy, know his ways, and learn to not be deceived by them.

You are more than a conqueror because Jesus Christ has redeemed you from all that and you stand on solid ground, the rock Jesus, and no wind or adversity can take you off that rock.

Day 28

I say sing unto me a new song. Do not say you have no song. You have the Holy Spirit residing within you. He was sent to indwell you and to direct you and to teach you. There is always a song within, you must only draw upon it and begin to sing. You will see things afresh and anew, so today is the day of the new song my child, sing loud and sing strong for it shall break strongholds and bondages the enemy has held you under for even generations. Today is the day to be delivered and to be set free for my glory.

How gracious He is to send Holy Spirit to indwell us and to teach us. Jesus was very clear when he left this earth that he was sending the Comforter. The Greek word for that is, *paraclete*, one who walks alongside, one who will be with and in you at all times. He knew we could not navigate this life without the third person of the trinity.

He (Jesus) is seated at the right hand of the father interceding for us and waiting for us to make his enemy a footstool for his feet in the heavenly realms. He knew that our song would be a weapon against the enemy's plan to defeat and destroy us. He gave us that song, so I challenge you today, good voice or not, sing that new song. Belt it out and you will so please the Father.

You will so defeat the enemy trying to take your song. He knows it is a powerful weapon. He will attempt to stop it. Do not let this happen, stand your ground.

Day 29

When my Word was being written for the ages those that were called to bring it about had no idea of the impact the words, inspired by Holy Spirit would have on people or the ages to come. Even though yes, my Word is the only word and will always be the only Word I am still speaking my inspiration by Holy Spirit through my people, and I have always spoken to my prophets first of what I am doing in the earth. But please understand that your words have impact. Does not my word say your words are life or death? Know that I am focusing on the words of life that you are speaking and need to realize that I am using you in this way to touch lives more than you realize. You will never know this side of eternity the impact of your spoken words. So take heed to speak life and think as you speak and ask me to speak through you.

He has created you to be a trumpet for Him and for His word. You have been given the gift to speak life into circumstances, into people, into regions upon the earth. You are His mouthpiece and He has given you the one that will guide you into all truth and will give you wisdom to speak what needs to be spoken, and to whom.

He has given gifts to enhance you and your destiny and to cause you to walk in levels of faith you did not know were available to you. Let today begin a fresh new page of speaking life, His word, encouragement, and peace to all you encounter. It is a very important part of your destiny to take steps of faith and watch how Father shows up on your scene and speaks through you.

Day 30

How easy it is for you to think that you understand by what you see with your eyes. Even nature understands the times and seasons. Each place in my kingdom has a time and season. And the sons of Issachar knew that they must be ready and know what the time and seasons were. In my creation I have set before you the understanding of spring, summer, winter, and fall. Look at these flags for understanding of what I am doing in the earth, whether it is in your life or in the life of a city or nation. Those that have chosen me will clearly be defined by their lives hidden in me. It is not in the place where all is well, at least with the circumstances, but like the seasons there is a plan and purpose for each one, and they must follow each other to the completion of the cycle and then there is a renewal and a starting over again of the seasons. My principles are not hard to understand, they are simple enough for a child to see, so see with the eyes of a child.

Understanding the things of the Kingdom is really not difficult; they were created to be ever before you and you need only to open your spiritual eyes and you will see. Like the biblical author who wrote about a man in fear who was having a difficult time obeying the Lord and did not think he would have victory, but an angel came and opened his spiritual eyes and said there are more for you than against you.

This caused the man to believe and realize he had an incredible army of the Lord right in his midst that would do battle with him and defeat the enemy. It is no different today. I promise you that there are more for you than against you and they are standing right next to you. Look with new spiritual eyes today and see the army of God sent by the King of Kings to do battle with you.

Thank him for sending them and for their help to complete this page of your destiny and the destiny of those around you.

Day 31

Do you not see the river that is running through your land? I am about to end the drought in your life. I am about to flood you with the rivers of living water, the water of life, the water that brings cleansing and restoration and refreshing.

It's true that quite often, less is more. In this case, this word is short and to the point and is full of promise and destiny. Jehovah is asking you specifically to see the river, his river, running through your life. A river running is first alive because it is moving forward, secondly because of that there are living creatures, from the smallest that can only be seen by a microscope to the big Salmon going upstream to fulfill its destiny. The struggle is great, but there is planted in its DNA its destiny and it will not fail because it is a created animal that fully submits to the will of God and to its personal destiny. Take today and study the Salmon and its life of faith and destiny which in the end produces hundreds more of like destiny. What a beautiful word picture of life and destiny and obedience.

Day 32

You are standing in the stretch of these 40 days and this nation is standing in the full throw of its greatest outpouring before Jesus returns to this earth to establish His kingdom in this world. We stand in the greatest time of history and he has selected us to be a part and to live in this time. That being said I would hope you would agree with me that now is the time of our personal visitation as well as this nation and the nations of the earth.

We have been created, like Esther, for such a time as this. We may think in ourselves "who me?" and the answer is "Yes you." How can it be? Well since he is Yahweh and we are not then it is his decision and we are the selected ones to fulfill His destiny in the earth and our destiny in our generation.

You are in the home stretch and you can sprint to the end because you have been equipped along the way for this very time. Let faith be released. Put your running shoes on for the finish line is right around the corner and the winner's circle is waiting for you to step into it and receive your reward.

This reward is one of many Father has promised to his children who endure to the end. Stand upright and rejoice for the day is upon you to receive His reward here on earth. You have done your homework, you have passed the test and you have said YES to his plan and purpose.

Day 33

Say out loud "God is alive" now let the words resound in the atmosphere around you. Do you believe the words you have just spoken? If you do then you know my child that I do not sleep and I do not worry, and I am all wise and know all things and have all things under my plan and it will succeed, like my prophet Jeremiah spoke that "I know the plans I have for you for success and not for failure" and that includes so many things that you are not even close to but seem to wonder if I have left the building. I assure you that I have not left anything or anyone anywhere and I am fully aware of all the enemies' plans to thwart my sovereign will. I have chosen to partner with you my church, and have given you all authority to trample on serpents, and scorpions, and over all the power of the enemy. Know that I will give you the ability to overcome because I am that I am and I will take care of all things and every scope and every group of people named upon this planet. The time truly is short and many things are looking as though I have forgotten, but know that you can depend on me and on my word and on Holy Spirit to guide and direct you in all things. Be not afraid, but walk boldly into this world being filled with the life of my son in you, with Holy Spirit indwelling you, and my angels surrounding you and helping you.

Declarations are one of the most powerful tools we have in Jehovah's kingdom. He has given us this tool to wield power over all the plans of the enemy. From Exodus to Revelation are passages where God's people declared or were told to declare the promises and truths he proclaimed through his prophets and people. You are his instrument of declaration; it is your voice that must resound to the heavens of what Jehovah has already declared. Remember our words are life or death. Let's declare the life of Yahweh and his word over our destiny and circumstances in our world.

To make known or to set forth is the description of what a declaration is. We are to make known to the powers and principalities the declarations of Jehovah's kingdom and to set forth his truth upon the earth, which will defeat the plan and schemes of the enemy.

When we declare something, we do so in the name of the Son, and the Father based on their words. We are leading out with truth that takes on motion and movement and change. It is very powerful. So today is a day to declare. You are in the last week of these 40 days of movement into deeper levels of your destiny, so go on and declare it to the heavens.

Day 34

Do you know how extravagant my love is? It certainly is not what the world thinks is love. My extravagant love is individual and it is corporate. It is something so strong and so true that the strongest thing in the universe cannot stop it. Its strength can change a nation. It can stop water from going forth, it can stop torrents of rain, and it can stop an earthquake. It can also be the driving force in a marriage that is on the rocks and will restore it. My love and desire for you is beyond what you have understood to this point. Today this day, this very day I want you to turn your eyes and heart toward me and receive, yes receive my extravagant love. It covers everything that you think is a problem, pain, and struggle in your life. It will stop the tide of your emotions and turn those emotions toward me and will allow you to become free, free in me, no matter what the circumstances look like around you. It is something that will not be forced upon you for it would be of no effect if it were forced. It is to be received, embraced and enjoyed and allowed to turn your life down a new street, a new season, yes even a new life. Remember love changed all of mankind forever when it climbed up on a piece of wood and allowed itself to be nailed there, and to bleed out there and to be the scourge of all because they did not know what love was.

We are all familiar with 1 Corinthians 13, "the love chapter." The words penned by Holy Spirit are in direct opposition to the world's view of love on many levels. And here Father is declaring over us his extravagant love, which is way over the top and is so deep and so wide we cannot comprehend it. It is important that we receive that love every day. Let today be Valentine's Day all day and look at every turn for an expression of your Father's extravagant love. I promise you he will not disappoint you. You will smile at each expression.

Look for it especially in the little things, the love of a pet in its eyes when you take time to pet or speak to it; from a child, any child and how they so exemplify the Father's love in their simple faith and response when someone smiles or speaks a kind word to them, even in the grocery store at the checkout stand. I believe you will be amazed. Make it a day to do over and over, watching looking and experiencing the love of God all day long. It will move you forward in destiny in quantum leaps.

Day 35

Today is your new season. And I will bring forth he harvest I have ordained since the foundation of the earth. Rejoice today as I open the storehouse of heaven to you this very day.

From this juncture having walked now 34 days into these 40 days of adding depth to your destiny we have now come to another chosen expression of the Father over you. You have realized that you have been chosen, by the creator of the universe, to express his character, his life, his word to all of your sphere of influence.

You have been created for such a time as this, and whatever season you are in right now will transition into the next season, and the next season, and the next, and then you will begin them again but with new strength, new revelation, new faith, and new understanding of what you were created for *His glory*. You have been hidden in Christ in the heavenlies. Christ is seated at the right hand of the Father interceding for you each day. He is intentional about you fulfilling your destiny.

Would you write a letter to yourself today about this journey and where you have come from and what has been revealed to you? What are some of the experiences?

How your destiny has been moved forward by your commitment to these 40 days. Give it to someone you trust, and ask them to mail it to you in 1 year from this day. Take your time, you might even find a small remembrance that will fit into the envelope to remind you of this time in your life.

Day 36

Do you not see the river that is running through your land? I am about to end the drought in your life. I am about to flood you with the rivers of living water, the water of life, the water that brings cleansing and restoration and refreshing.

I have waited long enough to see in this land what I have ordained since the beginning of time. It is Alpha and Omega time, it is Kairos time for many who have waited patiently and prayed unceasingly to see my hand move. My hand is not slow but I have waited for the time of the ages to stretch forth my hand across this land again and see revival fires begin to burn and to ignite many cities and towns across the landscape of the United States. I have in my hand a sickle that will cut down anything that gets in my way, for the harvest belongs to me and me alone and it is time for the sickle to bring in the harvest and the tares that have remained will be thrown into the fire of eternal pain and suffering. It is yet time for some who have yet to surrender, call them in during this hour and watch and see what I will do on your behalf. See with the eyes of the Spirit for I am watching and I have my hand raised the time is now and not tomorrow but today.

This land is two-fold. First, it is the land you walk on, this land of America, or whatever country you live in, but even more important it is you. *You* are this land He is prophesying to. It is time for the hand of Jehovah to move on your behalf and to revive you in areas you did not even know needed reviving. And for a fire to be rekindled where you thought the fire was out, no embers, doused with cold water and never to be ignited again.

I am sure you have some areas that need surrendering to the will of Jehovah. We all do,. The hand of God, that which is more powerful than anything in the universe and beyond has lifted it up, to release to you untold mysteries, untold revelations and untold destiny that will leave you speechless.

Make this day a day of discovery. Write in whatever you have chosen to write in, this book, a journal, your computer, whatever two new discoveries you have realized at this juncture of your 40 days which is quickly coming to an end. Also look through these 40 days for key words that stand out to you that are repeated. Of course destiny is the key word of this document, but find others that stood out to you.

Make a plaque, or fabric art, or computer art or whatever, or find one manufactured and place it in a significant place where you will be reminded of it and of its significance. Also put the date on it so you will remember when this had an impact on your life. My desire is that you will complete this "Mission Impossible" assignment if you choose to, and it will not self-destruct in 90 seconds, but it will instead have a long-term impact on you and those you touch in your sphere of influence, no matter how big or small.

Nothing is insignificant, and nothing about you is insignificant, in fact, you are far more important, valuable, needed and significant than you have realized. By this point you should be able to realize that. Look back again at what the number 40 means and apply it to you right now because it is real and you have been diligent in your pursuit of adding depth to your destiny. You have pressed onward and upward and have succeeded, no one fails this class, and each person passes the test and gets a gold seal of completion and a new upgrade in your spirit.

The drought is over, the rain clouds have gathered and are about to dump on you a deluge of the rain of heaven and it is glorious. You can dance, you can sing, you can jump and shout for the rain of His spirit has been poured out upon you and you have climbed the mountain, and stand at the top, stronger than ever before. And if you look closely you will find some new and stronger and bigger spiritual muscles that you did not have when you began this journey.

You go Rocky! Wish I had the soundtrack to start playing as this juncture, but you know what I mean. Begin to celebrate. You are only a few days from completion of these 40 days and you deserve to celebrate, and do not do it alone, find someone who will celebrate you and your victory. We all need to find places where we're celebrated.

Day 37

SHIFT...SHIFT...SHIFT... can you feel it. I am shifting things in the earth, yes across the entire earth. Look to the earth to declare what I am doing in the Kingdom of Heaven. I am shifting the earth in places it has never been shifted before. I am shifting things in the nation of America I have never shifted before. And yes, even the world and those who have turned their back on me and my grace, will begin to see with their eyes what I am doing and they will stand in terror of what is before them. Watch the earth and listen to what is happening deep within the earth and watch and see what is happening deep within the oceans of the earth. There is a major shift in the water that will take place very soon, even in the next 30-60 days; it will even be announced on CNN. I have not been waiting for the sake of man I have waited for the sake of the Kingdom and those who have not bowed their knee to me, in giving me their lives. I am not lacking in my concern for what is happening across the earth in peoples' lives and in my church. I am waiting on souls that have been ordained since the foundations of the earth to come into the kingdom. It is a time for a major thrust for intercession for the souls of man to come to Jesus. Yes, the time is short, you must, my children, raise your intercession, cry out for the salvation of many who are on the doorsteps of hell and they do not even know they have *chosen this path. But I am God and I can change the hearts of man. I need you to pray for the veil of unbelief to be removed. And I need the veil of unbelief in the church to be removed. For many are standing in pews even now and think they are secure because they are in the house. But I declare to you that YOU are the house of God, YOU are the temple of the Holy Spirit and I will not be contained in the buildings of man. I never have and I will not in this hour. Run to the streets my beloved, run to the nations and cry out for the souls of people being weighed in the balance right now, even nations being weighed in the balance. It is the Hour, it is upon you, NOW, NOW, NOW the Kingdom of God has come and is even in you and before you and around you NOW. The Market Place is waiting, yes I said waiting for the sons of God to come to them and love and draw them into my presence, for miracles, even healings of Aids on the streets to manifest before men of unbelief. I will have my church and I will have it the way I have intended it to be for generations and generations. I have been waiting long enough for the truth to be revealed as a wind blowing by Holy Spirit across the land, lands long ago laying destitute because of the choices of man in nations that are even now spiraling down to the depth of evil and destruction and even an opening in the earth that will swallow even like the days of Korah. See my hand is outreached and will not be removed for yet a short time and I will bring salvation to many who you thought would never come into the Kingdom of God. Many have waited for this now time to be revealed in the earth.*

Watch the children rise up in your midst, watch them begin to manifest their childlike faith and my power in them. Do not worry about their understanding, it is my faith released upon a generation like no other in any other time. They will be the generals of the day in this hour and you will be amazed at their faith, their integrity and their destination of destiny.

It is truly a time of shifting, and you have and are being shifted into your new level of destiny and you have been positioned by Yahweh for this hour of need in the earth. You are in his hands and your feet are planted, across the earth and right next door in your neighborhood. As I have said before, do not lean on your own understanding. Put your faith and trust in the only one capable of shifting things and watch with him as things around shift into their rightful positions, including people you have been praying for.

You have come to the kingdom for such a time as this, like Esther. She was a young girl, with no understanding of what was happening to her or what was required of her. She listened to Mordecai, her wise relative who she trusted. From that place of humility and no understanding, she led the way to the salvation of the entire Jewish nation, the children of Israel, the chosen people of Jehovah. The principle is still the same and there are many Esther's (male and female) rising up to their destiny in the earth. When everything around them is shaking, they will not be shaken and they will not topple, because they stand upon the rock Jesus, and not on shifting sands. You cannot be moved because Jesus Christ has you secure in His arms, and Holy Spirit is right inside to direct, protect and show you the way

You are coming to the end of these 40 days with new hope, new faith, and a new energy and plan for the days ahead. I honor you for your diligence, your perseverance, and your faith to set a goal and complete it, *hurrah for you!*

Day 38

SALVATION is waiting for many in this hour, many across the earth, whole people groups, groups that have known me in a measure and in this hour revelation will lighten their way to the full path of eternal life.

This is you and many others that have known Yahweh in a measure, but others like you decided they wanted more. What a great desire to want more of the Kingdom of God and to be more than you were before and to see the measure you have lived in up to this time. Take a huge jump into greater measures.

We each have been given a portion, have been given gifts, depending on so many factors, all important, and none more important than any other. Receive your portion today, activate the gifts Holy Spirit is giving you, and thank Him for the things that factor into your personal destiny, because this is all about you and *your* destiny. It is not about another person or place but smack dab the spotlight is on you and you alone.

Step into that spotlight and receive your due reward for your due diligence, your diploma. It is one of many, enough that in the end you could probably wallpaper a room with the diplomas you have received. Some of them may be forgotten and need to be remembered, they are all significant and all are the 'seasons' and timelines of your destiny in this life you have chosen to live.

Celebrate *you* today and your upcoming graduation day in a few days, and find someone to share your journey. Find someone you can help begin this same journey in their life. You could gather a group together and lead them in doing 40 days of adding depth to their destiny. Why not? You did it, and your success will help them succeed.

Day 39

When my Word was being written for the ages those that were called to bring it about had no idea of the impact the words, inspired by Holy Spirit would have on people or the ages to come. Even though yes, my Word is the only word and will always be the only Word I am still speaking my inspiration by Holy Spirit through my people, and I have always spoken to my prophets first of what I am doing in the earth. But please understand that your words have impact. Does not my word say your words are life or death? Know that I am focusing on the words of life that you are speaking and need to realize that I am using you in this way to touch lives more than you realize. You will never know this side of eternity the impact of your spoken words. So take heed to speak life and think as you speak and ask me to speak through you.

As we are quickly drawing to a close of these 40 days of destiny please take very seriously the value, importance, and impact your words have. Destiny is moving you forward and the words you speak will have impact in whole new ways. Take seriously what you speak forth and be encouraged that Holy Spirit will give you words you did not know you had.

You will release them over people and speak life in places where death is trying to take over a person's life and steal their destiny. Know well, the enemy of our souls not only hates Jehovah, Jesus Christ and Holy Spirit but he hates to see people walking in their destiny and changing things around them by the abiding life that is within them.

You are a driving force for the Kingdom of Jehovah and there is no stopping you because you have Him who is able to do exceedingly, abundantly, above anything we could dream or ask inside you. Additionally He who began that work in you will not stop and promises to complete it, as you walk day by day with Him. His promises to you are yes and amen.

He will never leave you or leave you stranded but will always come to your rescue. He promises to get you out of tight places and places you have gone that you shouldn't have gone into in the first place. His promises will find a way of escape for you. He will hide His word in your heart so you won't make wrong choices, and most of all, your sins are forgiven. He has washed them in His precious blood and nothing you could do can change your position in him and your security in Him or the salvation He has brought you and me.

Your 40 days of destiny are right around the corner. It has been an honor to walk it with you and I would love to hear your story. I am as close as your computer screen at *www.destinytraining.org*, our Facebook fan page, or personal page. Post your journey for many to see and learn from and be encouraged by your journey.

This is not the end, Volume Two will be following down the road a bit, hope you find it in your local bookstore (ask for it and they will order if they do not have it), your internet bookstore and take the next journey with me and your destiny.

Take some time here to jot down some bullet points of importance you have learned, heard, or experienced in this journey; it will help you remember and it will help others that you will lead down this same path.

-
-
-
-

Day 40

Oh how I long to see you walk in the fullness of what I have created you for, your DNA in the kingdom. If you could only see what I see, the wondrous anointing of Holy Spirit awaiting for you to walk in a freedom and confidence that supersedes anything else that tries to tell you that you cannot do it. You are capable of greatness, capable of the miraculous. Do you not remember you are my child with my DNA, my anointing, my confidence? Rise up this day and look straight forward. Do not look to the right or the left and take that step of faith, today, not tomorrow, right now, and see what unfolds before your very eyes. Walk in my spirit, not in the flesh, walk in faith beyond yourself. Faith is not faith if there is no trying without knowing. See today, it is that day which I have longed for to see you in my majesty.

Well the day is here and you have completed what you began 40 days ago. You are a different person than when you began, I am certain of that fact. Yahweh's word says listen to the prophets and you will prosper. You have for 40 days heard each prophetic word, read it, meditated on it, and believed it for your own life. As a result you have prospered and will continue to prosper.

You are walking in new fullness of your destiny and your godly DNA. Freedom and confidence have increased, and the greatness of Yahweh is more evident to you than when you began. I know there have been miracles throughout this process and they have forever changed you, and will change others also. Your faith may have been renewed. At least I know it has increased. You have taken new steps of faith that you never thought you could, but you did. You believed Him and He met you the moment you took that first step of faith in each new area.

Continue to walk in His spirit. I am sure you have come to a better understanding of the flesh and how it will take you down any old path it can to fulfill its desires which do not agree with your creator.

Father says over you He has waited for this day in your life and he is pleased and he will watch you continue to move forward and grow through many experiences that he will put on the table of choice for you to pick from. They are all good, but each one has a perfect timing.

Pray for that timing before you embark on any new choices. He will again show you the way, and make the way, even when there seems to be no way. He is the Way Maker. So go forth, your destiny has increased and your fulfillment will continue to grow as you walk day by day in this glorious life of Christ.

Bibliography

Holy Bible, New Living Translation ®, copyright © 1996, 2004 by Tyndale Charitable Trust Used by permission of Tyndale House Publishers. All rights reserved.

Interpreting the Symbols and Types, Kevin J. Conner; City Bible Publishing, 1992 Portland Oregon.

The Prophet's Dictionary, Paula A. Price; 1999 Paula Price, page 221

American Dictionary of the English Language, Noah Webster, 1828; Foundation for Christian Education, San Francisco, California.

His Glorious Names, Rev. Qaumaniq and Dr. Suuqiina; IMI Publishing, Victorville, Ca.

About the Author

Dr. Candi MacAlpine's main purpose is to impart wisdom and truth so that you can be released to fulfill your destiny with integrity and excellence.

In 2009 she strategically launched a 24/7 international prayer room in the heart of California. She has been trail blazing the Kingdom for over 40 years. Her passions are leading prayer teams into nations for transformation and breakthrough; and discipling individuals.

She founded *Destiny Training Center* in the heart of California in 2000 and continues equipping the saints for the work of the ministry through her books, teaching, and prophetic CD's and DVD's.

Other Books Written by the Author

Take Back the Night

Peter the Pebble, Peter the Rock,

The Journey of Our Destiny

www.ingramcontent.com/pod-product-compliance
Lightning Source LLC
Chambersburg PA
CBHW070543300426
44113CB00011B/1774